PETS ROCK®

THIS IS A CARLTON BOOK

First published in Great Britain in 2016 by Carlton Books
A division of the Carlton Publishing Group
20 Mortimer Street
London W1T 3JW

Text and design © Carlton Publishing Group 2016
Images © Takkoda 2008–2016

Words by Joel Jessup

Printed in China

A CIP catalogue record for this book is available from the
British Library.

Editor: Charlotte Selby
Design Manager: Russell Knowles
Production: Maria Petalidou

ISBN 978-1-78097-755-3

10 9 8 7 6 5 4 3 2 1

PETS ROCK®

More Fun Than Fame!

CARLTON
BOOKS

Introduction

What do you imagine your pets are up to while you're out of the house? Sleeping quietly on the sofa? Waiting patiently for you? In the Pets Rock® world – with their owners away, the pets will play! Let's face it; our pets have a lot more spare time on their paws than us. Time to fill with a bit of dressing up and getting into character. Living their lives vicariously through the glamour of celebrity. The costumes may be perfect but the behaviour isn't quite there! Just what crazy cosplay antics are these feisty pets up to? Turn the page and prepare to learn just how much... Pets Rock!

"Guinea pig played superstar."

"In theory I know all
my relatives."

"One feels one should stamp one's authority...
First class or second?"

"The puurfect accessory for the little black dress? Cat hair dahling!"

"We're such a close couple; people refer to us as Cog. Or Dat."

"I'm trying to build an online following, but so far all I have is fleas. I call them my flealiebers."

"The most important things in my life are rock, charity and that guy in my cage who looks exactly like me except he's flat and shiny."

"Take the picture quickly; my owner
needs the tea towels back."

"Bones: we will bury them on the beaches, and in the back garden, and in the neighbour's flowerbeds..."

"Not tonight, Josephine."

"God save the guinea pig."

"And you will know my name is Mr Snuffles
when I lay my paw upon you."

"Who wants to see me swing on a giant hairball?
Hwwaaarrk."

"A lot of people think I'm fake, and I say, well obviously: I'm wearing a wig and a costume."

"As an immortal guinea pig I have lived for almost seven years! HA HA HA."

"I'm always rockin' and rollin'...
in things that I shouldn't."

"I'm not so much a painter as a panter.
Depends on the weather really."

"The Buddha teaches calm in all things. Except for when someone even slightly touches your food bowl, in which case go nuts."

"I want you... to let me chase that cat from number 64."

"My ideal revolution is a 360-degree roll over in front of the fire."

"We're supposed to be brothers
but come on..."

"People say I have a voice like a bird. Could be the chaffinch I ate earlier. It hasn't gone down yet."

"My gravelly voice is just the
result of a hairball."

"Alas, poor slipper! I knew it well. Several times. Then buried it in the garden."

"I've joined a gang... well, it's actually a kennel club."

"I love to paint spots on every animal!
Except the already spotty ones.
I paint stripes on them."

"Cats and guinea pigs in the same band? Whose idea was that? There used to be eight of us..."

"Mirrorballs... Cat discos are a nightmare!"

"I'm trying to be as elegant as possible but sometimes you just can't keep the litter in the tray..."

"Eight out ten cats prefer diamonds."

"I'm more a working 11 'til 11:15
kind of girl."

"They say I talk with a bit of a drawl;
actually it's a bit of drool."

"I was being a silent movie star, until the postman appeared at the end of the front path."

"Carrot in your ear, peanut up your nose?
You wanna eat more sensibly!"

"You should try getting in and out of the cat flap in a wig. Not easy."

"Cat Beard be the name!"

"Only problem with the space capsule is you can't stick your head out of the window as you go."

"The king is in the building. Now he's left the building. Now he's in the building. Oh man, I'm so excited the front door is open!"

"I saw a grey hair and thought
I would dye!"

"I've got five dead mice under here."

"Four score and seven meows ago,
our paw fathers..."

"I've been looking for a tiny human to come on my travels but it's not easy."

"How about a smoothie?"

"I believe in the power of the herb.
Cat nip."

"I've had 10 billion views.
Thanks, Mum!"

"The only things I can magically produce are small and brown. The act's not very popular..."

"Beware of the dog."

"When I said cut, I didn't mean
my portion."

"When the big dog barks, people listen."

"I got a shot... for the fleas."

"I spend a lot of time near the catwalk. Sometimes the temptation to chase is too much."

"Been rapping since I was a kitten. And by rapping, I mean coughing up hairballs."

"I deduce that the culprit who ate your
steak is... me! Sorry."

"I love putting on concerts, particularly at 4am outside my owner's window."

"I ate the meat costume before
I could put it on."

"Smelt like tinned spinach.
Yuck!"

"I am a rock god! No wait, a rock dog."

"I've found the fishnets are actually
useful for catching fish."

"I'm the lead guitarist but I'd rather be
the off-the-lead-guitarist."

"I think of myself as the father of Pup Art."

"Time is running out for people
to recognize my genius."

"I don't grab my own crotch. I prefer to jump up and sniff other people's."

"People think we live in a gilded cage. Actually we have two gilded cages; they put us in the other one when they need to change the straw."

"One more dog biscuit – that's an offer I can't refuse."

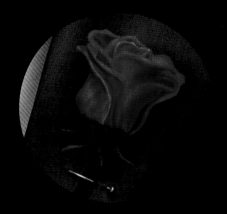

"No darling, not a possum, a guinea pig. And if you were half as smart as me you would have known that."

"Hail, Caesar!"

"I love a Caesar. Especially the anchovies..."

"All guinea pigs go to
heaven too."

"Quit your barkin'!"

"You barkin' at me?"

"I'm a cat-flapper from the twenties."

"We are not amused. We are, however, open to a game of tug of war with your new leather gloves."

"I gave up my acting career for a place on the throne.
Now it turns out I'm not allowed on the furniture!"

"It takes me
a while to get
into character.
And the outfit."

"I've tried bathing in ass's milk while getting ready but I always end up drinking it all."

"I've stuffed my cheeks with cotton wool. Actually, it's two hamsters."

"Don't make
me laugh;
my mascara's
going to run!"

"This afro
requires a lot
of combing.
See you in
14 hours!"

"That naked selfie has come back to haunt me."

"The jewellery is really heavy. The collar and lead is a lot less effort."

"If you think you can look more fabulous than me, you must be joking."

"We might be cat and dog but don't believe the rumours."

"I'm used to playing multiple roles. Just don't let my owners know my secret."

"Thank you, thank you very much. Now where's my peanut-butter-and-jelly-filled bone?"

"A cat's gotta do what a cat's gotta do. And afterwards, you gotta clean it up for me."

About Pets Rock®

Launched in 2008, Takkoda's award-winning brand Pets Rock® is a striking play on our enduring fascination with pets and the cult of celebrity. "Takkoda" is derived from the Sioux word meaning "friend to all".

It is the brainchild of a London-based photography and design partnership run by Mark and Kate Polyblank. Mark and Kate's passion for design and detail coupled with their interest in story-telling led to the development of the unique world of Pets Rock®.

Mark and Kate usually take photos of the animals in their photographic studio or otherwise photograph the pets in their home with a high-resolution camera. After that they draw absolutely everything – each individual hair, jewel and accessory – by hand using a digital program. Every part of the image is created by them from scratch.

The Pets Rock® phenomenon has spread from its London base to leading UK stores and on to a global network of licensees and retailers whose customers are barking mad for their furry friends.

With more than 75 characters in the Pets Rock® world and many more waiting to be let off the leash, you're never far from one of their pop culture pets.

"YOUR PET NEEDS
YOU"